27 Carolina Avenue
and
Other
Allusions

27 Carolina Avenue and Other Allusions

Selected Poems

James Robert McNally

Copyright © 2007 by James Robert McNally.

ISBN:		Softcover		978-1-4257-6286-5

All rights reserved. No part of this book may be reproduced or transmitted in any form or by any means, electronic or mechanical, including photocopying, recording, or by any information storage and retrieval system, without permission in writing from the copyright owner.

This book was printed in the United States of America.

To order additional copies of this book, contact:
Xlibris Corporation
1-888-795-4274
www.Xlibris.com
Orders@Xlibris.com

35059

CONTENTS

1. Gaps 9
2. Tales of Gods 12
3. Terror: Before & After 36
4. Hands & Knees 37
5. From 'Dubya' to 'W' 38
6. Quia IX XI MMI 39
7. Ponderings of a Trapped Soldier 40
8. Encounter with a Caravan 41
9. A Truth Discovered Before Dying 42
10. Painting of a Horse 43
11. And Great was its Fall 45
12. Onward 46
13. Bill & George 47
14. Carlton 49
15. Pennsylvania Avenue 50
16. The Terrorist 51
17. Ruben Soto 52
18. Come to Ol' Baghdad 54
19. Hinges 55
20. Gefilte Fish 56
21. Shards 57
22. My Wedding at Borders 59
23. Water 60
24. In Peru 61
25. The King of a Small Castle 63
26. Uss Ranger in Port, 1983: Subic Bay, The Philippine Islands 65
27. Heaven 67
28. Turning 68
29. Up is Down 71
30. The Journalist 72
31. Wife 75
32. 27 Carolina Avenue 77

Afterward 79
Notes on the Poems 81

To my wife Danila, a greater inspiration could not be wished for.

In memory of my father, John H. "Jack" McNally.
1923-2006

1

GAPS

From gaps in piles of rubble I saw him,
A young boy heading toward us—my men and I.
And he was carrying a package
Or a box . . . or . . .
. . . A bomb?

Eight years old, nine, ten tops, he walked while his lips
Juggled the directions his mind repeated to him.
Kids that young forget things, and kids there get in
Trouble when they do
But he walked

"We have our orders," I heard through outrage. "Now do it."
"He's a little kid," another voice equivocated. "A baby."
"Anyone in the circle. I won't say it again," the first voice iterated,
And yelled "stop" in two languages then in the direction of the lad,
Who had already looked up at the noise, made by his
Comrades' attempts at becoming au fait with probity,
And straight into my gaze
His were among the most beautiful eyes I had ever seen
The thin-brown of syrup before its slow descent into the
Pores of a still-warm stack of pancake

They glowed, I could tell—even from the eighty-six meters
My gauges told me was
The distance that separated us—with the kind of enthusiasm that would
    one day
Make people say 'yes' to him, and cause others, more
Available to that sort of thing,
To believe in miracles
Women, when he was a man, were going to give him what he wanted
And pray only that they could give him more

This, I evaluated, in a spare, bare-naked second

That reprieve, which endured
Discourse, ended when the blast of a
Single shot reported a stereo of echoes

How could it take more?

And one of the eyes that had been looking
Up at me was cast back over
The boy's shoulder, and searched
Through the rubble, that had been his
Town, for one last piece of fluency.
Eternally lost in thought

The other eye
Had been taken through the
Back of his head
Which had shattered before he even
Began his descent into the debris he had now
Become a part of.

The book, he'd been given
By those who hoped to set his mind
As free as we were making
His country,
Fell by his feet.

It's pages flailed
In the taut wind as if stricken and screaming
At the assault on their lord
Until their flapping fit became deafening

I wanted to hide but was pulled by humanity to stay
And by deeper obligations to focus in dishonor and humiliation
And so I stared out at the boy and his book
Until, I was certain, we had all gone mad
Or would soon
I thought I could read the pages of the book as
They fought back the wind in tortured repellence
They told me I would never return whole
That I had lost my privilege to love
That monsters on the path of righteousness
Were monsters still the same

Then I was stunned back from that opposing insanity
By a girl a girl I saw through a gap,
Who was wrapped in a sari.
She could have been his slightly older sister, and she was closing from
One hundred and thirteen meters beyond the body.

She seemed to be clutching a package, perhaps deceptively.
It was square-like and could have been . . .

TALES OF GODS

**To my dear friend Hal Sieber,
the better poet and finer man**

Eli, Eli, láma sa-bach'tha-ni?

A Game of Words and Distractions

The day's ends have gleamed too long,
Came the brash assessment of
The neo-cannon barons and mortar moguls
And the huddled lots who lived beyond the dusk.

But the Prophets, a plucky but ignored bouquet of observers
Who charted the determined slippage of light, became aware,
As did judges, that amid the intricacies of this dim caution,
We would finish in darkness.

So talk arose of a kind of vapid absence of light; where hardened men weep in
Places of trepidation and chronic dispassion; where joy is
Found in suffering habits; and hushes are
Released through gnashed teeth and nods.
Toasts there are offered to the whores of glory and victory is
Meted out in spurts of blinding blasts and disguised nostalgically.
In sum, a living darkness was born that bottom-fed on
Tiny glimmers and sparks before they grew too large to swallow
Or too vile to regurgitate.

Men walked in carpetless corridors where the echoes of footfalls
Ambushed anachronisms, called tradition and patriotism,
And other aged ideas.
Truth hid in nooks behind the stately columns adorning
Three-and-four deep office suites,
Which found gloom and chill even in summer's longest hours.

Idealism of their caste extended the length of their arms
During tiring handshakes, and, on the sunniest days,
When a future calm was envisioned, they focused entirely
On the storm that preceded it and
Sought the umbrella-brokers and levy-builders
And made mental notes on
Deals that could be made between them.

And so while light still radiated blindingly,
Before the tales of what kept it fluid were shattered,
The eyes of these men beaded, then leered, then ogled,
Then gathered and stored the radiance where they could.
But taking light they knew, in truth,
Was only part of making darkness
So, under the smoke-soaked rampage of a new reflection,
They assembled vocabulary reformers.
Darkness, even for this band of shadow-dwellers,
Would be difficult to deliver to those who understood light.
And word merchants would learn to earn their keep.

A new meaning of illumination, therefore, was
Contrived and presented to the early rising conclave.
The captains and colonels of this neologistic union—swore against the ranks of
The shadowmakers, castmongers, and bleakinstallers
Beneath the bright lights
But praised them on the altars they had been commissioned to erect—
Wrote that newlight (alternately called 'goodlight')
Would first fall on the vaunted 'enumerated rights,'
Which came to be counted and perceived as only
Those contained in the body,
And some of the 'enhancements' recently, thereupon it, made.
Badlight (sometimes called 'oldlight' or simply 'light')
Was turned on all other rights and
Began its gaining dissipation and otherwise
Dissention into the dungeon of a terrifying, hungry, and
Murky monster.

Ideas and individuals like cant, Kant, can't, and cantos
Interchanged so that philosophy, hypocrisy, indecency, and diversionary tactics
Burned on the same candle wick
The calm (called "whimsical" by the profligate decriers of it),
Draped eccentrically like vivid, wet silk,
And felt extravagant; an
Unearned indulgence,
An undeserved reprieve.
"Peace, peace, peace" was the call then.

But, as patriots before them bewailed,
There was no peace, and, those listening knew,
There never had been.

Artificial frost froze tongues to flagpoles,
A child's hoax that grew with little perception
Until the waging of waggings had become unseemly
And the jokes dissembled into plots and hatchings.

The drop in ambience, too, had caused the
Scribes' pen ink to lop off in chunks, clog the flow, and
Dam the stream.
The pool collecting there quickly attracted
Impurities and all constructs of adulteration.
While focus was elsewhere the
Contaminants cultivated, morphed, and,
Despite denial of the very science,
Evolved.

A statue was made of liberties.
But dual-intended or catchy headlines were,
By then, blasé and overlooked, while
Ambiguities of other sorts were enacted into
Law and could be made use of only
By those with clearance.

Imposing words, too,
Like skullduggery, debauchery, pandemonium, sedition, and provocateur
Had arrived at a renaissance, and were leaked, by high-brow imposters,
Upon those whose imagination conjured various definitions for them.

Horror and its synonyms were all that
Remained fit for reading.

Few stories on the misfortunes of the hawks and their hawkers attempted
To stimulate the sleepers-in and, with passion, stun
Them from this repose.
And these tales were concealed deep inside.
"*Not long ago I had both god and son,*"
A mother was reported in one of them to have cried.
"*And I'm left now with neither one.*
***My boy was taken from me, and my poor god has died.*"**

The Coming

Visits—in the patois and dialect of the new language—from those of
Higher worlds, in that pale and churlish year,
Were hatched, ordained, prescribed, dictated, and
Bellowed in blatant ploys, in blathered voices,
Misidentified or deposited, for, those who cared
To gaze upon the parade of their arrival,
And delivered in a thousand other, largely sordid, ways.

As shells fell to no purpose and the petals of
Flowers, shorn and scattered in just such a way as to mark
The path of the *liberators*,
Lie frozen and lilted in gardens where
Miles and meters mingled and
Taunts went unnoticed, apparitions unsolicited,
And ire—tediously—unsuppressed.

But the ghosts came by other names, and arrived
Always from the left, as if the masked
Antecedents for death itself derived
From the dead language for "kind" and "untasked."

Poets harkened to romantic times and
Scribbled odes to the cyclical nature of humanity and
The cynical ways of its protectorates.

Covens, courts and congregations gawked
With varied expressions of approval and awkwardness.
The Sunday preachers brandished copies of doctrine, intoned in garrulous and
Garbled ways, double-checked notes, consulted with more learned men, and then,
As did Moses with his carved code, and Caesar on his public
Hurled the new lexis of distorted tidings
Down upon the worshippers, whose minds and souls had
Moved more precisely away from things less ineffable.
And those same cloaked men cast curses on all others.

'Rex Americana lucta est; causa finita est.'

The weekday fare was less verbose and volatile and
Included the black-pen cartoonists capturing all the
Rampant executions of prayer and power; the blithe
Delegation of privileges, and the little-assailed abridgment of candor.
Housewives hung the renderings on their refrigerator doors
For their tired husbands to chuckle at.

God, or those speaking on his behalf, saw that time was being wasted.
There was so much to do . . .
So much . . .
. . . To do, they told us through vague and still vaguer interpretations,
That, when viewed from above, and at once,
It became impossible to endure.

And, many there did not
And most here refused to see the signs.
There were none blinder than they.

And prayer, while spoken about in ad hoc speeches,
Was either unemployed or failing badly
For days passed at a less laboring pace then the labor itself.
And God's people could do little to stop the swirling minutes

Or those caught inside them.

Meditation as powerful as comas
Could be tried except even less would bear it
And none but those in the planning rooms had time to attempt
It, and they had been exempted
From the need.

But talk of the all-knowing moved to the unseen and
Conversations of this type mixed unwell with weapons
Not unlike the blending of military acronyms and patriotic platitudes

The words were stifled finally, in more
Cunning ways than was the Baptist.
While the visible presently were presented as were the
Beasts who stirred the Divine.
And the non-synoptic teller of good news
Spoke of non-love infused with non-hate.

"If the world hates you," the odd John
Placed on the lips of the one once promised,
"Know that it has hated me before it hated you.
If you were of the world, the world would love what belonged to it;
But because you are not of the world, but out of the world,
The world hates you."

And the words were fleshed out, so was is written.

Loathing palmed off as affection, though, was a
Trick few presently dared attempt,
In this time of vital odium.

Saviors were in abundance then, catching one or two each perhaps,
But they were very few now, and love was an echo in the wilderness, similar to
Songs played long ago on the radio to combat the hatred that rung,
From the god-fearing and the god-addled, by the godless.

Which helped explain why other Johns were saddling up,
With paintings of cacti in the shape of crosses, and
Murals that included bushes and other, rarer and more stunning
Flora, hanging on their stable walls
As poorer horsemen and hangmen rode on creatures divined
In netherworlds and places few have walked through
And almost none of the brave even knew existed.

But we carried 50-pound packs
And, as the maggots we were told we were,
And those creatures less than these that we had become, did as we were told.
College degrees now far from our thoughts and less significant than
Celsius degrees, still we recalled the promises of tuition as they
Now reeked of blood and dripped of fouled intuition.

The dust of Jesus clung to us and, though unwelcome,
Would not be shaken.
We screamed for our deliverance from it and
For our mortal words to collect and
Impress those we had come to save, but
Village after village closed their ears to our message
And none made room for us to rest our heads.

Every day was another door
And every passage ended seven lives.
Our nightmares included latches and hinges,
Locks and the creaking of gates,
And we woke each day more tired
Than the one before.

Elsewhere, mullahs convened to defend their positions
On the reasons of their origin
Or how the Prophet's didactic was intended on his kin.
Was Ali the master, and, therefore, Muhammad's designee
Or merely just the great man's friend who stopped along the
Way to paradise?
The Shiites and the Sunnis, like the Irish, have used precision
On locks, slicing and splitting and picking
Hoping Gabriel would intervene with meaning.
Some day, praise Allah, all know that truth will come again.

Meanwhile, in the still,
Silhouettes connected and the
Tête-à-tête of such taboo table topics, collected into schemes,
Below the hush.

Then came the march,
The loud and bloody March.

Janus, with less ephemeral-minded gods, laughed
And Cried.

Material of Odd Weavings

The bright cloth
Contrasted with the haze and camouflage and the three thousand
Shades of grays and tans kicked up by the rolling convoys and
Melding, in an unsettling but too familiar way, with the
Smoke of fires—those both real and those
Only spoken of—and the dust of lengthy dying.

Truth, said to have been courted about in beaming shrouds,
Became a miracle that only the true believers
Admitted to seeing
And that only the truly blessed understood.

Then the garment became the argument
To the remaining classes, those seeking dates and documents
And other proof,
With which the spokespeople, said to be guardians thereof,
Were unwilling to part.
For, they said, God would rather it be another way.

God, for his part, grinned in an awful way,
At the cloths the material had been woven into and the
Flagpoles on which believers witnessed its waving.
It was a look that suggested he was shocked by the, now thematic, affair.

Then he thought of a way to impart Himself
So as not to deny the
Will of his creation
Nor burn holes in that
Which did not really exist.

Forms and Amorphous Leanings

God stayed in hiding for weeks
Until, that was, the varying forces banded, ecumenically,
And called upon Him to proclaim his side.

The masses cringed as His answer took a form
That seemed to belie versions offered by His spokespeople.

Some, whose protestations had been shunned, were now
Looked upon to decipher the clouded messages, which,
To many, had appeared in things that passed.

Others from similar groups translated the findings.

Those who spoke to God regularly were disappointed that He,
The All-Knowing, had disseminated His great code
Via margins of thin books and
Sans the smallest word of a sermon.

Those who had heard God's voice
Said the God others were hearing was bogus,
A conspiracy compared to those once put together by
Their friends against their enemies.
And those who were once beheld as merely loud now
Rejoiced in solemn ways, but
Still were able to
Drown the droning machines of intelligence.

The Month of Sorrows

April,
Once, exultingly ordained, the cruelest month,
And now just ominous and unwell and dim, planted
Dispossessed might into once-holy ground; indicted
Artificial foes with excepting sins and obsessive creeds; redressed
Corporal wounds with corrupted blood; shunned
Protests of discernment and discretion inside a passing fashion of integrity;
Desecrated internal and eternal cathedrals
With bright palls in dank and guarded strips; blocked
Bright passageways of truer understanding and
Seams of sanguinity with zealous weirs.

Winter chastened the yearning; nurturing
Metaphors into plausible intelligence
With fêted piety and coiled canons and tyrants
Plucked from wells; quenching
Yens with filtered sludge culled from nearly dried veins and the
Burnished fruit of fouled orchards
Until starvation and other forms of decay mattered more than death
And of foes, who resembled the allies of allies, around austere tables.

We trod our Vias Dolorosa, our paths of sorrow, us line of fools
While the brawny heat taunted us with
Curious but curative traces arising, from the
Euphrates ancient juices—in which Hammurabi tossed the anarchic,
Forged mud into bricks and pressed upon them
Laws now long ascended, and where Alexander

Baptized an empire—in hesitant mists from a sleeker Tigris—which Constantine
Churned, and later bridged and, later still,
Gated the ingress of the
Firmament—cleansed us, in spirit if not in flesh.
Thoughts levitated—Christ above the temperamental sea—
And contemplative fuel was spilled quelling flash-fires of peace
Flaring, on occasion, from brief eras of silence.

And then we drank what we could find,
Bathed in our boots, and made basins the way
Quixote imagined sacred helmets.

A hundred kings held the wind in their hands there
A thousand gods, born beneath them, plowed endings with curious
Shrugs, created truth with nods, and
Gathered equals from the ranks of those beneath the angels.

A million swords were forged and plunged defending them all
Floods blended with the sands and stones of their bloody graves
And other arcs grew upon the new land
While the ephemeral swallowed all its gloried imposters.

The scarred and scared and sacred fall
On the words of lessers now
Failings commingle now so gracefully with victory
Until each is the same and that is devoured by a third,
Less simple construct, that shall remain forever nameless, as
Weapons speak and elders stand muted.
Subtraction here is addition there and the numbers are tallied
By contractors whose uniforms, made in Italy, stay pressed
And whose coffee aroma fills the driven limousine
Which takes the bumps so well

Mortals have they all become.

But spring was summer there
And it brought too brief a forgetfulness of things, as thus,
Conjured up voices we would never know again.

Then, shaking dust and evidence from shards of soiled Arab affluence
With the sun, at the edge of the human record and
Spangled in nearly unbearable influence,
Bribing us to toast, with stale potion, the occupation
And diminishing brilliance we shared.

This assertion of the early heavens took my fears for a time
And I was moving with brothers down a hill on sleds in the snow-quilted
    woods.
"Turn or you will crash into the briar patch," they would scream too late
We called the collection of thorns and dead branches,
Where those not rudder-savvy enrolled, the wasteland.
We didn't know what that meant then.

We do now.

Yet we looked west, ever west, and remembered in the accounts;
The leathered horses and the muskets drawn protecting riches
Encased in glory and examined with fondness.

And still a knowing came to me that
I would not survive this ruin, this skeleton of justice,
This loathsome link, this
April.

Titles of Trees and Other Dying Things

With that often overlooked third branch
Of the sacred bush seeking
Higher ground, and warmer climes,
The remaining and newly labeled 'twinity'
Traded turns culling and calling names from
The elect—a precept that had apparently died
On the floor of a cathedral constructed mostly of glass—

Yaweh—called *Shem Hammephorash*; The Explicit Name;
The Separated Name; The Name By Excellence; He Of The Great Name;
The Only Name, The Glorious And Terrible Name,
The Hidden And Mysterious Name; The Name Of The Substance;
The Proper Name; and the once unpronounceable name,
Who was cried out upon later by the Son,
In the more simple terms of Father and Eli—selected first.
And the bidding wars were set in motion.

Other, lower, gods, steered free of this,
Having, as they did, little knowledge of saints (and having once been
Accused of misapplying the practice of martyrdom and sacrifice).
These gods also desired that their domains remain uncluttered.

Few mortals were reading when their souls were taken
To stand inspection
(Cleanliness being an obsession of the most high).

Such preoccupation, it appeared, had vanished during the
Course of the occupation.
And so neither Blake nor Wordsworth, Dickens nor Whitman,
Frost, Faulkner, Hemmingway, Dickinson, Eliot nor Pound
Were ever seen, heard, pondered, or found.

Blazes, then blasts,
Then no sight, then no sound.

Then the Son was ready for the second round.

"The good news,"
The Son is said to have told Luke years before, is
"That the kingdom of
God is being preached,"
The news less good, in
Casual course he added, is that
"Everyone enters it violently."

Ancient Tales of Wonder

Mountains have been moved, yet Mohammed weeps
Forbidden castles, once reaching where the old man razed Babble's
Tower, are barricades, and the barriers that kept
Peasants busy praying for their destruction
Morphed into monuments of the eternal days to come.
Gated gardens of a million orders, genus and phyla—where Easter applied
Itself to the masses and songs sprung from spores of splendor—conflated
Into graves, where the infidel and the prophet, the martyr and the saint,
Like the camel and scorpion; the wretched witch and the cunning priest;
The beachheads of abomination and the soothing balm,
Became one.

The glorious mount of debris from other crumbled towers was
Immortalized and parts of it
Sold, in the manner indulgences once were,
As relics of the terminal forbearance and anachronistic mercy and
Talismans against the fear
That fell from all corners of the oval.

And bibles collided

And tales once told in secret languages
Were laid bare
And explained in open oaths and pains deeply hidden.
And bearded men who knew obedience to only the
Rules of paradise
Were motivated to kneel toward places not eastward.
And long walks were taken in short spaces.

And sinners rejoiced.

An Appearance of the Future

The purpurea anima Virgil boasted of lay slain
And parsed.
The once blue veins ran red until
Rivers like the ones feared by the pharaohs
Crested the levies.

And any prophet could have foretold
Of the coming wreckage and carnage.
But all prophets had been sequestered and,
Finally, in their solitude, the once
Romantic influence of their words,
While still alive with alarm,
Were amplified into a stilted affectation.

In the drama that surrounded their broadcast, all
Implication of their proverbs and
Warnings appeared synthetic, in an era
When man-made things were to be mistrusted,
And they came to be listened to only incidentally.

Tattered Attire

The wind joined
Us new friends, us neo-nonbelievers—or believers in things
Not long known—before our journey ended,
Hauling to our place, in its carriage,
Joys of its journey, and, amid the less kind components of its character,
Tastes of the ardors reflective of its past or
Traces of where it had not been well received.

It hung like a drawing in blue ink in a room of red on a
Wall otherwise bedecked in more earthen ways,
And tantalized us with its itineration and a
Hope of our, too, being able to move.

We peered, indeed leered, at the distance
At its bends, corners and other fractured, crooked and petrified perfections,
As if heaven had fallen just beyond our consumption.
And the manna melted regularly.
Then we looked again and the wind was taking it to us
In tiny pieces we imagined we were tasting.
And we wished we could remember how to wish.

Any remnants of the talent that took us here had
Long since evaporated until the sweat of it became our menu.

The swirl of wind, the bouquet of its new importance, and
The patterns of its smiles, crawled, like
Cheated caravans, across our faces,
Long seared and silt-laden and heavy with tics and spasms,
Until they too faded into their own arid wastelands.

One of us spoke about the coming days and then of
Times beyond, when that which is far away will be
Close, and then past.

And, times later, when all that will be is
The wind, the gusty and august,
The August wind.

A View of the Large

Near where the nothingness, that Mohammad
Told of, was replaced with sand,
Allah turned into mud and mud into men
Was a place, we believed, where truth divided those not
Found from they that never were lost.

And then truth itself split in two
Half of it went, in the older river fork,
Which emptied into the shoeprint lake of the slain giant,
And drowned a cold, mysterious death.

The remaining half was swallowed
Whole and nearly instantly,
By those who would have us
Believe giants still ran,
But whose feet had left little trace of their ever having walked.

Visions from Above

Angels angled for a better view of the passing
Of the monarchs and despots and others who forgot
Their places on the eternal scroll
They nudged each other in amusing ways.
And the feathers of their wings gathered in a heap,
Fell to the earth, and covered parts of it like the blood
Of pigeons and larger sacrifices in the Temple drain.
They recalled the time that God, their god, suffered them to visit the earth
And slaughter legions of His chosen peoples' enemies.
Some of the angels wept when the memories became too clear,
For death, and other endings, were
Events they did not fully comprehend,
Fear brought tears to all but the most resolved and
That which they looked upon appeared a crueler
Form of the blighting and smiting an earlier time.
But, again, the angels' understanding of mass destruction
Was but a distant memory and they had not been involved in
This sort of elimination process in several millennia.
Indeed, the earth seemed to them a frightening place
And they rejoiced that they were angels and that God
Had placed them in heaven
And that He allowed them to see how things progressed
When He removed Himself from lower matters.

The Advent of the Fat

Below,
Far, far below
A converging mass of a disparate underground, rose
And a group called the 'Erstwhile Nodding Elsewhere' gathered to save
The children, from whom they would later would run,
And give voice to a god who whose roars once shook
Pain from fire and thunder from stilled clouds, whose
Suggestions molded mountains and dreams carved them.
God, their god, watched and pondered his mistakes,
Then turned and bowed and sought out things more complete.

Songs rising from the long
Files pleased even the deafened.
Its chorus started months before,
When the ancient rivers were news to them.
Poetic and lyrically they arrived before time made clichés of it all
As drops fell between the chords,
Which only the blind could hear.

Days, when the tired of thought mined meaning from the
Cavernous fissures in the flatlands,
And connoted clarity from the blurred backgrounds
Where obelisks and other phalli abounded,
Were days when unneeded moisture could bring sordid relief.

And numbers inveigled each other until only
The most cunning found their way to the center.
But those brazen enough to stand for worlds-away truth
Were hung by their curved necks outside the booth in which
They were delivered.

And the gawkers allowed smirks to crease their faces at the
Seeming portents, for their only skills were those of Addition
And the present days had been given over to the practitioners of Subtraction.
It was an era when the multitudes were divided, and
Parish priests carefully calculated what homilies could still hold sway
Over which particles of their congregations.
How to speak gladly of abundance when deficits were so easy to see.

The loss of hundreds and thousands and billions and trillions
Were acceptable for the time
But those who knew God, their god, knew too
That time was a fleeting traitor and a transient messiah,
And that the time would come when Time was wearing the uniform of
Those assembling more meekly.

The ghosts of the lost lots would become ciphers
Of things they could not see again and of places they would never visit
And only in that instant, when the faces
Finally became discernible and, eventually, invisible.
And in that same hour, the silo where the grain was harbored
Would be found with its walls gnawed through
And that the seeds of the harvest depleted.
And then they would discover they had not forgotten how to cry.

But tears that fell were few and dried
Quickly on the wind-blown ground, for
November was unseasonable, and the
Changing of its colors was one of reluctance
So, in consequence, the calories carried by the
Weighty seemed less afflictive.

Pause was given to the many dieters and the
Children, with flickering glances,
Watched from the seats at their ubiquitous screened desks
While parents gathered regularly to decide what answers
To give them and then hoped for questions, that rarely came.

When the novenas quieted and the embers cooled,
At length, then flickered and the candle-lighters acquiesced,
November relegated itself to the common forgotten.

Scarce sunshine was forthcoming, but shadows clung
As the men secreted in a pile of the hidden dead
Discovered even death is not final,
And that dying offers little relief.

But death, having become subtly nuanced and not long examined,
Lingered, nonetheless, as the aim, until little else was more taboo
And fewer topics remained less spoken about.

Allusions and euphemisms contracted daily,
Unburdening to even greater lengths,
The nearly paralyzed popular party, and the small
Pockets of miracle-tooters, tabulators and otherwise restless.

The Prophets, having once been dismissed,
Attempted to concentrate their persuasion
But the gathering of so many so similarly attuned
Resembled the very horrors of the vision they had foreseen for all the others,
And they dispersed before talk of conspiracy could be heard over
The noise of their own ill-fated consortium.

The Prophets began to starve for lack of need, and in
Their emaciated state, were unpleasant to look upon.
Their begging became most unseemly
As the listening world began demanding that the fat ones speak.

And the din of this cry finally reached the fat people
So speak, the fat ones did.

Those who had used their mouths for things other than addressing
The masses and had, hitherto, used the art of
Gesticulation as their prime means of communication,
Were quickly trained in speech,
For the proletariat demanded it be so
(Or, so those who reported upon it were told).

The grass, browned on even the most affluent lawns,
Had been cut for the last time of the year
But those gods that attended to their roots
Were trolling for more penetrating cures.
And the fat people began mowing their lawns
As a means of building their endurance
For delivery of the long speeches and harangues
That the hoards now expected of them.

But the fat people found the work too hard, and
They told the throngs that the future would prove itself; that
The time was ripe for horror; and that those not
Thoroughly insulated (By which they meant,
"Not fat enough") would find sin too tempting.

And they told of plans to make amendments—
In the way of Tom Bowdler—so that
Sloth, gluttony and pride (and, implicitly, lust)
Would be removed from further sermons in which the
Notions of either idealism or integrity or
Infidelity or iniquity held primacy.
And they warned repeatedly against collecting effects
That could be misconstrued, and told tales about mysterious
Forces that were gathering
And fronts that, presently, were forming.

These spoken sirens and tacit summons to action
Were received in varied ways.
Those who had called for the fat men, however,
Delighted in these simple sermons
Uncluttered, as they were, with penitence, relevance,
Benevolence, justice, thought, or
Human understanding of any discernable sort.

And the fat men, seeing this divisive receptiveness
Did away with any future seminars
And put more effort into
Getting fatter.
And elephants and skeletons came to
Symbolize the factions.

But then the bones grew muscle
And the shells on the pachyderms thickened
Until shields and strength were all
Anyone would talk about, lest they appear as people they
Did not believe themselves to be.
And secret codes became the primary language
Of the land.

But we, not privy to those kinds of details or granted
The luxury of involvement in pertinent conversations,
Sought truth where we could.

We quickly learned it did not emanate from
The temporal but from the eternal.

Out before when the earth was well
When the day, retelling the sun, was too bright
We hunted shadows.
When shade was swallowed in storm,
We found the trees and rocks that cast them.
When dusk gnawed away at their images, we
Looked deeper, to the mountains, and, in the darkness,
To the stars.

Finally, inward—when mercy granted the reprieve, saw that we would
Never hold our mothers' hands nor behold the pride in
Our fathers' eyes, that we would never again see the curve in the
Snowtrail or feel the cool splendor of grass dew on our feet, id est, when
The brutal briefness of that clarity allowed scant moments of
Delight—was the focus of our gazes
But peeks were all we were allowed.
For those things we would never see again,
Like the stare of a roused Medusa,
Would turn us to creations that would not die but merely end
And death, as it neared, was less terrible than its once distant
And defiant and flitting mirage.
And that death was the very least this life owed us.

November, now personified, and once robust, humbled itself
For it had taken on much more than it ever had
And gathered less than it was willing to surrender.
And as its Thursdays came and went, so,
Ultimately, too did those things it once
Hungered for and upon whose thanks and praise,
It feared, it may never again have the strength to bear.
And, as it withered away,
Awash in the blood of self-flagellation,
Few pitied its passing.

That Which Really Gathered

If redemption arrived at all
It was, distinctly, both late and ironic, in that
Death made us, in the end,
Forget about
Violence, and devastation took us toward
And away from
Destruction.

Water became the
Fire that seared hatred into healing and
Terror into fright.

Dry warmth, in the places of the celebrated gods,
Appeared ominously cold to those drowning in undrinkable water
And thirsting in filth
And those with breath still in them expelled its saddened dirges.

A burp for an infant god, barely conceived, still miles within the
Womb, and eons from delivery
Took tiny souls down
Closer to him (or her).
And, upon their union, he or she—for it,
As it were, remained neutered—neither
Celebrated nor scoffed,
For gods of this sort delight in
Resilience and shirk less enduring matters.

Many of us have died and, hence, not met so
Great a standard, and, though regaled in
Accordance with our disparate places,
Not learned the lessons taught
By the retelling of such grand accounts.

But other gods, now relaxed and old,
Appealed to a rustic lust for rumination.

Calendars were struck and torn
But future renderings of it would show that
Septembers (when men tinkered with heightened fear),
For countless tellers of terror, would forevermore be
Augusts, when those powers which govern its disposal
Told, with the airiness of a stretch and the forethought of a snigger,
Of horrors that lie beneath

And above,
Gods spawn and incubate,
And wait, without
Location and fully unannounced,
To visit.

3

TERROR: BEFORE & AFTER

We all know what terror was before
The Boogie Man, the tight-faced nun and Linda Blair's
Possession; the days before an oral; *The* War
We knew would never end, and budding pubic hairs

But now it's ambiguity we dread, pregnant with ambition
Bearded plotters lurking everywhere, awash in ammunition

Sharks; the shore at dark; and the undertow that could carry us
Away, were scary things to ponder. Our fathers getting a lay-off
From a job he hated but we needed; dread that ugly girls would marry us
Or that we'd never wed; my bed and that dreams would never reach a payoff

Now our leaders give alarming speeches
On how long and vague the bad men's reach is;
Tell horrid tales about how our beaches
Are not the happy places that their
Calming waves would seem to teach us

So we take cover in our homes and keep our ears
Clean, because no one knows what bad is anymore
Children are shielded from reliably pliant fears
Beneath the patting hands of parents and a flag nailed to the door
Monsters and devils live, they're told, and they have notable careers

4

HANDS & KNEES

Fingers,
Dipped in the new blue holy water,
Pointed to the place
God made His first appointments
And then they closed
And swung around.

This alteration in liquid hues
Followed, by hours,
The forming of cues,
Under shelter from showers,
And, by days, weeks and months,
The arrangement of smiles to shine at the news
And the disbursement of dues,
Paid in an off shade
And apt to ooze.

Visiting hours,
A period of time long debated,
Ended.

Prayers—
Entreated on calloused knees
On mats torn from feed bags
On ground littered with sand scattered from
Three continents, none of which they'd known much about
On an island ruled in ways that reminded them of a home
They would likely only see when their knees were worn completely
From cages dogs living half as well as them would feel imprisoned by
To a god vilified by witnesses—
Went unanswered.

FROM 'DUBYA' TO 'W'

You ran on a slat-thin morality and lazze-faire platform
(While those who knew you well smirked and chortled)
But on your slate was the sequel to Desert Strom
You said he was no Clinton, and, by way of hintin'
We assumed that meant you toked *and also* snorted

George, they call you Dubya,
—Let all your subjects your praises sing—
It's no wonder why your smile and eyes are shined up
And all the silly people lub ya, but did they have to go and dub ya
The boy still not so bright who would be king?

You said you were sent by the angel's bosses
Or other gods or voices heard while lost in thought
Then you substituted words for what you said were losses
(Of notes and lists of all the things you missed)
That apparent prayers and obfuscating silence bought

But, George, Dubya might disrespect you
(And, let's face it; there are plenty around to protect you)
So, perhaps to stand for Unaffected and Un-aficionado
Shall it make us warm to call you 'Double U'?
And try to forget all the trouble you
Didn't mean to let infect you
So many, many (well, not that many) years ago

QUIA IX XI MMI

NEW WARS ON OLD DUST

"For man is dust.

And thus arose the type that any man could trust.

From mounding mountains of grisly debris
Ruptured ghosts a-gallop into history.
But the simmering shifting of that volcanic woe
Became the smoke of recasting from things we know
Toward a vile incubator where small fears grow.

Uncommon was the delivery of this grave crime,
Which commingled with gravity and TV time.
But purveyors of this old and musty weight
Need not have left more than sampling freight
If not for a desire to resell their hate.

Presently fouled air is ubiquitous,
With loyalists seek emulsion in remnant dust,
While reeducating subjects on new meanings for clean,
And purging brightness, from posters, like sky-blue and grass-green
And posting banners and ribbons, and dark drawings of the fiend.

New dust now moves in from the once-staid west
Above sand-holding secrets of sins yet confessed
Mixed with the waste of what we've yet to learn,
And burst-filled songs and prayers to burn

". . . and onto dust man shall return"

PONDERINGS OF A TRAPPED SOLDIER

I don't know what happens to what's poured into a truck
After homes are lowered and roads are being built, or
What becomes of leaves that gather in fountains
Or how river rocks and sticks in streams become filters

I've wondered all my life how swirls of wind
Climb and carry seeds, and other acts of alteration,
Inside their pockets, jingling there with coins of death
And, when silence reasserts itself, all accept their novel station

Saturated, I have been, by fluid self-reflection
(Confusion and misplacements have been like gods to me)
And things that most have glanced upon with passing grace
I have studied, indeed, dissected, for their oddities

I have marched aside kings of social order,
Among artists of the screed and scrawl
Many times I've heard nature walking
Now commingled in my mind remains the footfall
Yet the chapels near the wars of love
House the soldiers of my mind's minute's congregation
Wading through repeated sermons on
Changeless truths and the sting of flagellation

Though still, at times, like the wind
Never has love been my very air
Upon which floats the mystic mixture
Named for she with whom I share

8

ENCOUNTER WITH A CARAVAN

The covered party chanced upon us, in our
Suppressing tans and cammies,
Before our journey would ever end in the place from which they came.
Heaving without effort, lugging without mercy,
Their collective mien was a mural of tales rooted somewhere beyond pain,
Beyond pain's seeking of forgiveness,
Beyond any redemption forgiveness may have supplied

I peered across the heat to the wealth they hauled
And saw, amid their burden,
A bundle of swaddled lavenders, vermilions, and cadmium hues.
I thought I understood a component of their stoicism;
That piece that cannot be given over to type, status or circumstances;
That agreed upon part, that uniquely desolate contract
Love makes with hate and peace with war and giants
With those who would chance all truth in defiance
Of it

Their journey, we knew, was interminable
And one we would not be ask to join
But the alpha nodded toward place were a barrel
Was carted inside a wagon, more deferentially kept
Then their colorful parcel
The present held eminence over the future
And immediate sway upon the past

We drank and filled what we could
While the caravan dissolved into the dust

9

A TRUTH DISCOVERED BEFORE DYING

"Tell them all," the soldier, with his ending breaths, said
Wrote the much-confused reporter for the rag
That any self-respecting right winger (who's not a Log Cabin fag)
Worth his semi-furled party pin has never read

Tell them what? the writer asked with fret
That the water in the rivers and the gulf are nice?
That the people need more books and rice?
Or that we are not even close to being finished yet?

His eyes vacillated wildly, then settled with calm precision
And found a balance, I supposed, that comes when guilt has acquiesced
And a million separate inner voyagers enrolled on a single quest
And the absolution, his look so recently betrayed, was replaced by a decision

Then staring beyond anything here he said, "It's not as we were told,"
Again, the reporter sighed and thought and drew the obvious conclusions;
That war's end rarely is, and, in this case, fear and alarum were less than allusions
"Love, truth and liberty," the warrior spoke as he died, "like life, can't be
    controlled."

10

PAINTING OF A HORSE

Trampled upon strokes, meted out in increments
By an inner voice caught in the canyons of lunacy
Tamped, but clear enough in denial to leave the senses unpenned,

Built, lash upon lash, upon a myth of manifestation
From a pallet of unseen instruction

Until, coal-hoofed and acquiescent, emerges
The smoky beast, wafting on a window of the artist wonder,
Confounds the fragile birds pencil-perched above
Whose freedom is too apparent for inspiration
Whose detachment is too tentative to pioneer faith, and whose
Bravery is too disguised by the omniscience of its restlessness to enlist

But oh, the black and mighty maestro of the mystery of the gait,
The tireless and tactful, nay, the genteel dancer of
The forest and the wood and the main
Whose simple trot could freeze our corporeal, fleeting, banal gaze,
Whose reigned but gracious nod,
Would arrest the wants of the pedestrian masses

The shiny carter of legions and legends, whose obedience to the
Vaunted crusader is reversed when its humble strength
Appraises, and impeccable allegiance salutes

"horse," spoken with a lack of due deliberation and with the
Head held low and the tone
Adjusted thusly, bleeds from the tongue garbled and unseemly
Lurks unfinished cheap, grotesque, and juvenile

But "*HORSE*" when given its regal bearing
And the inflected adulation rightfully accorded it,
Is nearer to god then any feeble human legs could carry us

Horse is the wind and we are its wake

Ignoring the streets of ash and walls of fire
Lying in a tunnel burrowed through all invention
It is us who are blinded by
Whatever residue rests outside that mire

Kingdoms have been lost for your lack
And mortals have been deafened by fiends
Heard outside your handler's crack
But many who have crashed the gates of hell
And heaven both, rode there, my rendered friend,
Upon your gracious, nay, glorious back

11

AND GREAT WAS ITS FALL

Who believed them when they said
It was exactly what we were going to need?
And who still clung to that same insanity
When it became clear the motive was greed,
And then went further, waving banners, shouting
About unity even after so many started to bleed?

It was us, the bobbling masses, who nodded and smiled,
And claimed that what was great for few was good for all,
Though some scorned this brigade who sculpted fear,
They were penned-in fiends with signs in left-hand scrawl.
And only cautious listeners heard the truth they shouted.
But the hollow followers knew this new machine would never stall.

But long ago a seer said he saw
A large bird soaring, which then went dead within its glide
It dropped, it is told, without losing its stride
And great was its fall

ONWARD

He limps.
He doesn't have to,
But moving fast and ably
Might help destroy
What he has labored to create.
Perfection belies its antecedents:
Pain, toil, the surmounting of deceit,
The surrendering of honor, the displacement of truth
The denial of agenda items.

So he crosses stages, ascends phases
And otherwise passes through
Armed with metaphors,
Along with hitches, hobbles, and shuffles.
And sometimes his fraudulent
Gait is rebuffed.
But, like the calling by a messiah to rise,
He now refuses to be told what to do.

And if his walk resembles a march
He allows that mistake, and limps onward.

13

BILL & GEORGE

We wrote, urgently, on fellatio
Queried short-term, turn-around, stock
Now we're flush with felons we'd pay to know
And it seems we've all gotten writer's block

Washington was blind, Jefferson was nuts
Worse were Madison and Monroe
Payne was a simple trouble-making putz
Adams and Franklin were just slow

Have we lost the way back to when killing was wrong
Indeed, lost our once brave feet?
Now even the signs and the protest songs
Are waved and sung from laptop seats

Airplanes turned buildings into hell one day
And sent leaders to the pulpits to talk of heaven
Then this horrible sacrificial display
Became their anthem, '9/11'

But soupy cigars and soiled evening gown tales,
Spin better than yellow cake stew
But just as there are rainbow trout and whales
There are liars and there's George W

Only ardent politico-philes
Would say Bill was more moral than Junior
Clinton's one lie made nervous men smile
Bush's are what they made Camp Lejeune for

So the son handpicks the ones who can ask
Of him the questions weeded out in advance
For while his sessions are more tssk than task
His handle-men leave scant little to chance

And not wishing to ruffle his new clothes,
He nakedly speaks bold nonsense.
While we delight in pretending he knows,
He grins and ignores our pretense.

But history dusts the must from old tombs
And old ghosts are waiting to rise
Though we may endure his mops and his brooms
Future looms with hows, whos and whys

We smell urine; he tells us it's raining
Says soft prayers while broadcasting fear
Sometimes, some matters need some explaining
But, secrets are why he is here

He won when the numbers said he went down
Got rich while his partners went bust,
Is always putting entitlement down
While protecting the family name's trust

So nothing at all is as it should be
If openness should be our goal
What good, Lord knows, in being free
If it costs us our once free soul

14

CARLTON

Don't go out like Carlton
When Ol' Lefty weren't the same
Keep your tread deep in the dirt
Someone out there might get hurt
'Tis war, not some goddamn game

Take the mound like '32'
His arm so strong and able
His locker stall a stable
His curveball off the table
And as deadly as the flu

Stay only as long as ye
Can, aims and skills do not be-
Smear. Wait not past the time re-
Lief's become your saving grace
And your love knows not your face

Keep a secret of a ball
That not another soul knew
You had. Smile when they call
And beg to tell them how you
Gripped the seams, release and all

Never let others have fun
With the way you've overstayed
Don't go away like Carlton
And ne'er pray the way he prayed

PENNSYLVANIA AVENUE

On Pennsylvania there's a cartoon telling phony tales
About the many things he's said but yet to show
And all the people who want to know
Are told where to go

Parents gather and throw taunts at his motorcade
But the cartoon laughs at them behind their backs
And then he rambles on about attacks
That were prearranged, very strange

Pennsylvania Avenue is not the place
To hear truth or see a single trace
Of honor, meanwhile back

On Pennsylvania there's a bald man with a cellular
And in his desk drawer is a long list of his schemes
He likes to take it out and talk in streams
With the other fiends

Pennsylvania Avenue has fouled the air
With sullied ghosts and godless prayer
We cry, but why, because

Behind a rifle near the entrance of a bivouac
A frightened kid is buying mercy for his soul
By selling all that's on his broken mind
And bartering his time

On Pennsylvania rulers take another measurement
And note the numbers, breathing hard, and then agree
That figures like this are never free
Who cares, seems to be the call.
Answered, let it be

16

THE TERRORIST

Scrawny eyes marking unformed smiles
Through lips no honest woman's kissed
And emotion stolen from the crocodiles
With brow a-furrowed and hands a-fist
Came the first words uttered of the terrorist.

Miasma bolstered their crystal creeds
As fighters of battles, declared in mist,
Landed in codes as storms and steeds
While orders demanded paraders desist
Descent gave console to the terrorist

Truth, and miracles and mountains, sought
Tellers to bring the songs and visions, and artists
To convey the unassailability it bought
With pools of urine wine-from-water pissed
In the corners of the caves of the terrorist

Then odd men from strange places
Spoke openly of war and a secret list
Alluding always to the runners of races
And mentioning often the terrorist

If he has a beard and speaks weird,
Are you getting the gist?
Don't panic too much, if your security's cleared
Information is needed on the terrorist

RUBEN SOTO

Songs of Ruben Soto, tranquil,
Damned from sides of which he knew none
And captured with an empty gun,

Echo beyond the taken hill

A boy, his jailor, reminded
Ruben Soto, who removed him-
Self from childhood; vital, trim

That, at end, he'd never find it

He did, but loathed the doing, and
Saved tears he'd later need for sweat
While learning the need to forget

Yellow bones burned into black sand

Ruben, born border grade, restored
Fast from howl-hidden hunger pangs
And myths like starlight's mystery clangs,

Sought urns from which his life was poured

"Soto," bellowed out the bathtub-
Middled, khaki-pleated monster
After seeing his signature

Finding for him a floor to scrub

Then Ruben marched and crawled until
His eyes blurred, freight seared calluses
Deep inside him, and chalices

He thought he sought had reached their fill

A book Ruben ne'er saw before
Told of salvation for the true and tried
Talk of his own echoed through the door

Inside the hour that Ruben die

18

COME TO OL' BAGHDAD

From Johannesburg, South Africa
Where shows on peace appear in hues
And in the French Quarter
So badly drenched in Russian water
Fly from Moscow, if you choose
But come to Baghdad,
For the driest time you've ever had

Oh, the gardens no longer hang but intertwine
With the crater roots and treasure left behind
And fig leaves can't stop quite enough sunshine

From Lima, Peru and Timbuktu
And eastern Michigan near Kalamazoo
From Camden New Jersey, on the Delaware
From Zurich, hop a flight on Swissair
And, lest you suffer from mal de mer
A boat 'cross the gulf can get you there
The water, sky and land,
Though, are thick, salty and quite bland
And every one and thing else is just damn sad
Come though, por favor, to ol' Baghdad

But there is still a thing or two a man can find
Who's lost most, but not all, of his sane mind
Along the streets between the towns that now are lined

With killers who pray to live and pray-ers who have had
One too many chats with the friends of friends in ol' Baghdad

So come and discuss
On a steel-shielded bus
See if all the fume and the fuss
Is just a fancy or fad
Or what passes for progress
In ol' Baghdad

19

HINGES

Where were you when
The hinge became the door
And it slammed, damn tight
And kept out all the poor
Then the rain-wrought rust rotted
Motion from its moor

What was your chore
When tape became our windows
And doubt became our core?
Were you sure
When our souls became our sanity
And fear became our lure,
When we forced all understanding
To seep, like fog, in through the floor?

Whose side were you for
When the hinge became the door?

GEFILTE FISH

Understanding is never owned
Rather borrowed, at best adopted, or dabbled in
Like finger food during the High Holidays
When atheists take in the ceremony
But smirk at the deeper meaning.

The cobbled seafood still must be eaten, however,
And the questions need answers nonetheless.
So the youngest inquires of the day
As if the sun had fell from it.

The elders then talk of demons defeated
And the deserts in which they died.

This is truth, or the seeds of it, some of which are sprinkled
On the food that only the wise speak of
And only the tongue can
Understand.

21

SHARDS

The villagers sleep at last
Dissenting notions all are stilled
The lords and lorded have found their castes
Invading forces have been killed
Tempered links build stronger fences
As droves haul statues from the yards
Calm voices speak well of violence
While the hopeful cling to shards

Water, though, is rising fast
Ascending houses, halls and hills
And striking such a stark contrast
To the chalky taste of pain-killing pills
For we talk a strolling comedy
Written, a-quill, by finest bards
But advance so delicately
And tiptoe through the shards

We recall love's perfect poem written at
A singular desk, in an ancient chair
That sold for a price what an astronomer, with the
Best viewing agents, would ever see beyond fair
But what did we care?
Nothing stirred our vision toward cost
The numbers working for us were too far ahead
Of those occasional foot-draggers who lost

The table set, the dealer dealt
We'd all end up with aces
The king, he showed us everything,
And we never saw jacks' faces

We now get by on worthless chips
And the table's flush with guards
We're kept guessing what the game is
Because we never see the cards

The king's in leotards
And his kingdom is in shards

22

MY WEDDING AT BORDERS

Dizzied wisdom cedes,
Stories begin, eyes attend
And café chairs still
While weary scents blend
With ill-practiced creeds,
A cured will,
And rousted sighs.
Enduring's cool council endorses
The concord of its age.
And vigor's courier complies,
While a gathering hush forces
Startled readers to hold their page
And the gruff instant to nosh its charge.
Books loiter, some advising the shrewd
To restrain, and, the less so to defray.
Long shadows stretch like a river barge
Wake, then dance with ambience renewed
By the relativity of the day.
She enters to a quieting cartel,
Shakes off a feigned smile then supplies
A forlorn expression searching for something of
Which it knows little, while her eyes
And bearing drink in the tone, and the smell,
And the early notes in a song on love.
We walk in unplanned scale,
Stop as if with landing gear
Start in focus, fade to stares.
Her sobriety and beauty at once prevail
As the crowd and place disappear
And neither of us cares.

WATER

I've trudged and drank and splashed and sunk in
Lakes and wells and streams and fountains
And rinsed my dried teeth and splintered tongue
With a handful of melted mountain

I've washed my face in middle-ocean mist,
Fallen asleep counting the raindrops I've kissed,
And rowed a crude raft with a pond-sullied wrist.

I've walked inside the sacred Urumbamba River's charm
In the valley of gods of intellect near the fort of a ghost's great arm
Then climbed into their heaven and moved the dirt of their ancient farm

I've carried frozen puddles in my young and muddled hair,
Ran along the earth's edge, nude, gleaning naught a stare,
And dove headlong into pools of wonder that were, really, barely there.

I once tested my sanity in a small ballpark cascade
And took in my sons like a hanger bay until the surge was stayed
Then disgorged through the vomitory inside the flood it made

But now I'm so thirsty I cannot even perspire
And when the worry of death subsides and I think,
My memories of water are my kindling fire
Now my eyes are so dry that it pains me to blink
Yet I would suffer the whims of a torturer's ire
If he left me enough strength to enjoy one last drink.

24

IN PERU

Ancient stone lanes miss
Impeccability by fractions of modern measurements
And repeat a map first
Etched in an Incan furrow
Try, try, try they do but never reach
The Quechua proposal for the wall
Dividing gods from worshippers.
The language includes no curses, inspires no slang,
Announces no consternation, recognizes no term for tomorrow
But still the signs of them are there, and those
Who visit are called upon to follow their way through
Between busy photo-snappers and the least and the priests
Along constricted streets, in taxis or on feet
In Peru

The means narrows near the granite fortress
While the seamstress whiles earthy hair into yarn
She is nearly blind to the
Bland arrays of eastern tones, deaf to western syntax,
Has squandered all but the raw edge of her keenness
And wishes not to cast the last of her senses impetuously
Or in ways upon which whims have taken others she once knew
She knows no one now
She sits, on a stool and pulls wool,
In Peru

David waves and smiles and sing-songs his
Way down a mountain through the curves of a
Bus built for snake-track road
He gathers watchers at each turn while his skin
Blends more brownly into the path he travels
He has fed whatever deities live on or in Machu Picchu
And if they exist, they are not just few
And now healthy gods feed him,
He is young and sinewy and slim
So, unlike the excess of the city side, there was no fat to trim
On neither one of David's is tied anything like a shoe
He just stops, waves and runs, like he was shot from guns
Through a jungle
In Peru

25

THE KING OF A SMALL CASTLE

The memory called golf his obsession,
Said his love was Bogie films, and beer.
But I imagined a side of him secluded
And thought of him more involved and far less clear

While I had no doubt
He'd trudge hills of snow
To permit, or purge, or pull, or push, or plow
And that his toil made tomatoes grow

He moved on magic clouds of industry
His motion made straight each troubled turn
He cared naught for odd or spiced variety
And never spent a dime he didn't earn

But to speak of him simply for his ethic
Would be to whisper words, which, out loud, need be screamed
And to hold that his life amounted to providing,
Alas, denied that he, indeed, had lived, or loved, or dreamed

As a lad, I saw an old and harried king
Held by a moat of wonder he'd refused
What he gave to carve his tiny castle
Included the cost of stones he never used

I bowed, nonetheless, at his great nature
Was beholden to his ways, stayed in his reach
But the awfulness and awe that most intrigued me
Were the thoughts that never made it to his speech

I feared him as the firmament fears the greater heaven;
The unknowing, feats of conjure; ships at sea, the wind
I knew him as the prayerful know their penance
He knew me as God knows those who've sinned

The statue, in the end, is not cut of ancient mystery
Worn away, but of cooled truth chiseled to release
And the shining sum of life is hardly shards and sparkled dust
But the memories time fashions into love and peace

26

USS Ranger In Port, 1983:
SUBIC BAY, THE PHILIPPINE ISLANDS

I recall clearly the cloud-cover but have nearly forgotten . . .

Floating and wondering if there would ever be
More noble things then what they fought for
And sleeping and dreaming of real children laugh
And sounds that didn't echo 'general quarters!'

But still I remember . . .
Afoot on land where children
Dove for dimes in rat-infested waters
Kids, who never saw a Sam's Club or Sears outlet surplus store,
Had cowboy-lasso ragged nets, and busted cups and cardboard
Pirate treasure chests on ships of drift that had washed a shore

We walked above them, a modeled lot, like kings of France and Sweden
And looked past the crust of dives inside their eyes, then flipped coins
That splashed beside their cries and starving pander-pleading

I can still hear . . .

Young Tagalog voices, rising in stench, berating our aim from a naval force
 of sash-tied Former sellers' signs, now sewer-river vessels, built, one-each,
 with captain's perch
And pre-pubescent, post-desperate vying urchin armies equipped with black
 market
Memories, and stranded, generations deep, in the fetid murk of Rome's vast
 church

But we seemed scarcely swayed by these sonic prods
While the diction rubbed scabs off our fluid unease
Yet we left, as a cult greater blessed by purer gods,
And found other ways to repair our souls' disease.

Once over the bridge we were instant men
Bent on maturing things we'd remember when . . .

Oh, they lifted brief shirts on olive luring mounds
Grown downy pert for the occasion
Smiles stretched across each face
Like banners at the marketplace
Brazen wax-stripped dealers of deviant vacations

Ink, still wet on our fingers from writing grand
Grieving, lavish letters, forced balled fists into tight pockets
Where the coins we kept mixed nicely with our bands.
Minds filtered out the things we knew from what we saw
Deciding what to take and what to leave in foreign lands.

Tinged steam rising from the ghettos beyond the pier
And dollar-simple knick-knack fairs and monger-minion meetings
Where easy-discoursed meat-men to talk you from your fear
And nods from every black-haired head, attend dialected greetings

Diesel-drunk dark from too few recent miracles and
Walking inside waves at night,
Pissed-on things, when lit just right,
(And what I'd now trade blood, nay, flesh),
Cornered swinging doors on a timeless store
In which even stale and moldy bread looked fresh
Near gates of glory,
Where God's only son would surely be
If man's sins had all been paid for
And the road to heaven shined free . . .

. . . is part of what I saw behind me . . .

On an overcast day
On tour, in port, in Subic Bay.

HEAVEN

If I believed in heaven, I'd
Die, but would be quite
Unaware of the death I died
What, with my new world unwired
And, as my would-be fellow soul-siblings
Have often, as witnesses, testified,
God and his son, and half-earthly mother-surrogate
Would be among those in line at my side

If only the truth about life was contained in the
Words they sung, with arms waving, and have said
I have no doubt I'd have hastened the pace
Found peace and debriefed it, left it all and been dead

TURNING

When I turned 15
The sloppy green
Was spilling everywhere and
The tight air did its all to hold it in

And I'd run through the woods trying
To break it down
But all I found
Were even greener questions and their marks
Kicked on up the paths cut into the barks
And covered me with green so warped
It bridged its own darks

I came close I thought then, but would not find
The place existing in between,
The world and all the its green

And green, anyway, from what I'd seen
Is not a good lesson to a boy
Turning 15

Three years later the world was blue
But paint schemes
Did not exactly derive from dreams
And yet we did what young men do
Everyone then was old but me, inclu-
Ding people I never saw or knew

Turing 18,
I was a bit bony and not quite as mean
As the others who determined to
Find there way through
Alone, on Navy stew and beans
Is a tough time for a man
Turning 18

By 21 I understood I was young
Again and I started plying my youth
And playing this game I would learn was truth
The rules were whatever fell from my tongue
Say, for example, I'd lost, well I won
For less than I recall, it was kind of fun
But trapped, I still was on this island,
Called Turning 21

At 25 I took the dive, left the plane
And broke the clouds and caused the rain
Sought the secrets of breathing when water rushed
And rode me and pounded my sense, crushed
All my understanding and left me wasting, nearly whole,
My hard-earned carefulness on another soul
Who was barely alive
Yes, I walked the aisle
When I turned 25

Triple X, without the sex
Leaves only scene after poorly acted scene
And scripts no director actually expects
A real actor to strictly follow
The structure's base and hard to swallow
The plot is patently obscene
The dialog obtuse and wordy
Perhaps there is a reason '30'
Doesn't rhyme with 'clean'

But oh I was so old then, as the old
Song singers sang, but my cold
Aging soon would peak
And my younger voice learn to speak.
Like a mad scientist who finds a cure
To stop death, I found the door,
Not a metaphor,
And walked through it
When I turned 34

That was a decade ago
And teaching taught me I'm better fit to learn,
For while the pages of books
Will not turn
Me into anyone who even looks
Like a sage,
Each of them, each book, each page
Told me that age
Can add and subtract
To my journey, from my back

So as my fifth decade nears it mid
And I've spent years uncovering the mountains I've hid
I know now that life spins
And have left my gold box of truth
Next to the velvet bag of my sins
Of course I understand
They were once all one, and dividing them up
Accounts for most of my nightoil burning
There is a good chance I'll see them
Together again as I continue on turning

29

UP IS DOWN

Letting go of earth, I fall into the sky
A hole, deep in the ground, is where I learn to fly

I breathe in water and swim in air
And understand well all life on earth is fair
And my black skin gains me free entrance everywhere

"The road to heaven", the Master said, "is eternally wide"
"So sin," he continued, "for there's no lack or room inside"

I'm nowhere for which planning and fate have played roles
The winners are those who haven't attained any goals
And the deaf are startled when the alarm bell tolls

Prisons house only the wise and the free
And war makes perfect sense to me

I open my mouth to look into the dark
But the sounds land on my tongue and park
With my feet bound to a chair, on my journey I embark

I stand and rest my legs and back
Speak of peace while I plan my attack
And carry the world in a tiny paper sack

I write love songs for those I dread
Feed the planet with a loaf of bread
Make actionable harangues while lying flat on my bed
I call for the death of those who are dead
And believe every word every politician has said

THE JOURNALIST

Sits amid clutter searching his mind for clarity
While his
Fingers draw circles of parity
Which comes not from great thought but rather its passing
The writer of prose knows clichés and platitudes
Stand abreast tales and ambiguities
He crosses the hurdles of deadline didactics
Pays no attention to other penman tactics
The journalist is forever engaged in his practice

The journalist's dances is a banal ballet
And knows
His epic poem will be authored some day
But current perusers glean information incidental to learning
The journalist gazes beyond the
Gorges of insolence, banality and hyperbole
To that place where the haughty truly toast taciturn defendants
And kings and counts commingle with accountants
Where the eternal and ephemeral merge into neither
And the conscience walks on weak waves of permanence
He makes angles of abstractions from his perch the fence
The journalist jots lines into substantiation

The journalist nudges the wise but eschews
Their wisdom
His nostrils are filled with aromas of the culinary maestros
But he risks all on a taste of their wares
He sees—indeed is enveloped in—beauty
But yearns not its carnality
He grasps anguish yet neither suffers nor consoles
He breathes fouled air, contracts with bandits, and seeks out light in shadow
The journalist conjugates, juxtaposes, probes, grills and elicits

The journalist defines dignitaries and statesmen
While moving
Unseen amid those who defer to their fancied fortes
Like machines in the service of wars and sorties
The journalist strives toward the art of the ghost
Holds no place at the tables, tips not his glass at the toast
Dividing fiends from those who seek them
He know eight synonyms for every aim and action
But uses only two, nay, one
His heart and mind once ignited the fires
His pen now clinically stomps out
The journalist aspires to the poetic but protects that yen

The journalist knows the street and ponders
The world
But sees only sites with a tales a-need of tendering

And shares only those items worthy of note
He avoids the glib heroes or those who gloat
His humble notes belie their noble cause
The more ghastly the phrase the less he gives pause
His end is uninterrupted by revolution, revulsion or riot
The journalist's reputation glides on gale winds of transcendence
But while his faith rests in revelations of truth and minutiae,
He prays for the succinct

The journalist stores numbers and
Files names
Of those from he can extract fillers and background
And in a drawer in a corner are the
Special few he can track down
When the links between graphs have no segue
Then he expands on terms surrounding the gist
To compensate for the details he's missed
Both the monster and the master of pageantry
As does the dolt and doted on,
The captains and crews and the boats the floated on
In equal doses, disregard the journalist

The journalist can rhyme the phrase
"Halfway decent hack" with "aphrodisiac"
But poetry, he knows, can spur his degeneration
For the journalist, idle time bears a lust for things less prosaic,
But seconds comprise the border between afoot and archaic
The journalist is a glutton for truth, but unlike Pilate,
Rarely asks just what it is
His life is to construct an essay of a quiz
The journalist waste little time on the "ohs" and "ahs"
Rejects the notion that his words should give pause
The journalist leaves others to work on the flow and the flaws

WIFE

To my double-wife Danila

Wife is a marvelous term
That scoots around the mind and memory
Like a freshly unearthed worm.
It grazes in the lazy fields and finds
Comfort in cool ponds and solitude on splashed
Upon rocks in the canyons of the mind.

Wife, when alluded to in whispers, is a benign,
Peculiar tag, headings in a gilded anthology
Of ocular vacations and watermelon vines,
Dogged-eared pages of the uniquely preferred,
An evolution lived out in labs of laps and porch chairs.
Wife is hardly a sufficient word.

Wife, even Prufrock would agree,
Is an escaping escalation into vastness and
A slipping, perhaps, on floors too clutter-free
There will be time for inadequacies and doubt
And taking in the language, now waiting in invention,
And multiple impulses kept from getting out.

Wife contracts with diamond carnivals, underwear
And phallic connotations, while hopping
Across the hammered-on in hopeless disrepair.
Wife, the good one, knows the strength of dealings did
In darkness or misdeeds in any tone of light
Propels what keener eyes blur, stronger souls forbid

Wife believes in acquiescing but her trust
Resides in ideas made real in resignation
She holds hard the deal of the undiscussed
While letting fall a calming sound or phrase
Wife pays homage to minutes as they unfold
But slight undue admiration for the fleeting days

Man could, alone, discharge the passions of his life
But autonomy disperses when he is honored by his wife

27 CAROLINA AVENUE

A knock is barley heard by near three-dozen ears
On an over-smothered sofa, a reluctant place appears
As the youngest set of legs scurries to the door
Allowing entrance to a freckled face most there hadn't seen before
Hardly a pace inside the house, the new feet are anchored to the floor

And the new mouth goes agape at what the new eyes do behold
And the visitor blinks them often for her mind remains unsold
Talk, oh yes she'd heard all that about this family's numbing number
And rumors contained every account of what such a count might encumber
But this sea of souls was laid out like a river moving lumber

As every pair of eyes recasts themselves upon the new arrival
The visitor looks jittery and awash in thoughts for her survival
But she refocuses and forces something normal to her bearing
And seeks like made to find the one who placed her in such daring
She nods or bows and reemploys her wits and tries to shake away the staring

She clearly needs an exit plan or the energy to remain
So she says, "hi" to me, and through my siblings I seek a lane
While her countenance moves from distance to one filled with distain
And I suddenly wish she would outside have waited
For I know, after her observing me *in situ*, how our friendship was fated

Outside we walk, neither knowing what to say
Now actors in a far less than comical play
Measuring how much the last few minutes would weigh
After traveling almost the full length of the street
She glances at a house like mine then down to her feet

"These are four or five-people homes," she says to the ground
And I know I have lost what I only so recently found
I take the first step toward her—as she continues—then turn around
Profound thoughts come as I walk slowly back up Carolina, a bit sore
At the conditions into which I'm about to re-enter and its attending corps

I wade in thoughts amid my menacing ghosts, as they emerge from my arching
Disappearance, and, conflicted about returning, I stop and watch ants marching
In the kind of grand, bland intricate innateness that dared not interfere
With us and passed over our home the way ancient dancing fiends stayed clear
Of certain eldest sons in smaller family circles, held more heavenly dear
Questions arose like, 'is it my fault?' and 'is it anyone's else's worry?'
And 'is it right to blame?' and 'should I look for a hatchet to bury?'
But it's home, I say inside my mind, the confessor that absolves the sin of worry
The '2' and '7' on the pillar-post bring me (or as close as figures can) to ease
And wind that sneaks around the pink tin shingled frame is an ever-
   curing breeze

Still I stand and look, from out, into the house and I hear the rising conversation
That scales a million walls and dies a thousand deaths, then hides in dread
   frustration
I then hear a laugh begin and then it grows and grows into its own creation
And I look up into the dusking sky, and its impossible prompts toward heaven
All of which seems a strange road map down Carolina Avenue and straight
   to '27'

AFTERWARD

There is little in these poems that makes any sense, but there is even less that isn't perfectly obvious. I believe that duality exists not only in poetry but in everything, both physical and imagined. We see or believe in something and make an assessment of it. Some dig deeper and find the roots, the hows, the whys and their attending affects. But even a baby understands gravity. She drops her bottle once and realizes it is no longer in her reach. She drops it again and understands that it has gone closer to her feet (though she may not understand her feet fully yet) and not closer to her head. As the baby continues to drop her bottle she will eventually glean as full an understanding of gravity as most 20 and 50 and 100 times her age will ever grasp.

But even as banal a discovery as gravity, at its base, is, most people will be victims of its rich and absolute lack of forgiveness in different ways—falling, dropping things, etc.—and that uniqueness will define gravity for us. Even a physicist, who parses gravity to its molecular particulars rate of acceleration will know gravity best by the scar on his elbow or the broken picture frame on his desk.

That is not to say that we must live every experience in life to gain full, or, indeed any, knowledge of it. Few of us will fight in a war battle but we can still appreciate the horrors of "Saving Private Ryan." And almost none of us have had to make "Sophie's Choice," but we all can relate to what a brutal decision one like that must be.

Conversely we have all loved; our lovers, our parents, our siblings, our children, our friends. But is there a universal love, just as there is a universal meter? And even if such a thing as love could be qualified or quantified, would my love be your love?

And so there are the poems.

Meanings can jump out at you, the reader, that even the poet did not see or had no intention of proscribing. Are these meanings wrong? That could depend on the phenomenon of poetry as a medium. If the poet is adamant that elephant is a metaphor for mundane power and audacity, and one reader is certain it represents willowy existentialism, and another that it is not a metaphor at all, who is right?

I think there are three answers to that.

If the intention of the poet is to send a definitive message, perhaps he should not be so ambiguous as to place an elephant in a poem in such a way as to allow it to be understood so vaguely when he wanted concision.

In this scenario, the poet would need to tidy up his work.

And this would also include the idea that poetry is simply a one-way means of communication (i.e. the same as writing a letter).

From another view, if the poet intended an absence of clarity, and gave the elephant two or three or more distinct or possible meanings, one for each of the layers he hoped the poem could be read on, there is still a sending phenomenon going on, and the poet is still very much in control.

In the third scenario, the poet selects the elephant because it could be many things to many people and he leaves it for the reader to decide. In this case, the poem is a receiving phenomenon, not a sending one.

And so I offer you some of my poems. Read them as you like. Some are simple some less so. Your tasks are to find which are which, but your pleasure is to take from them those things that will make you a more complete person and leave behind those that may detract you from your journey.

The ideas I lay out in explaining this poetry are not necessarily the only ideas that can be culled from them. They may not have even be what I was thinking when I wrote them but only the way I recall the experience.

In either case, enjoy.

J.R. McNally
March 20, 2006

NOTES ON THE POEMS

One: *Gaps*
This is one of several poems in this collection dealing with the insanity of war. To wit; he death of a child carrying a book, which could have been a bomb, but wasn't. This poem points at the price humans pay for taking on the savage role of soldier and killing machine.

The poem's last lines, of course, are there to point out that grief brings neither relief nor remorse and helps to show that the craziness of causing death cannot be ended by human suffering or human understanding so long as humans lose their humanity.

Two: *Tales of Gods*
This poem is a response to the theology of revenge that seeped into the sensibilities of most civilizations millennia ago. It is now rooted and perhaps, in light of what we now know, even more ridiculous than ever. To explain this poem in detail may be to take away from it. Suffice it to say, if you believe something about it, it is.

Three: *Terror: Before and After*
This poem was written in response to the hysteria created and maintained following the events of September 11, 2001.

Four: *Hands and Knees*
A glance at the elections in Iraq (in which digits of voters were dipped into blue dye to help curb voter fraud by allowing voters to cast multiple ballots) and the tortuous treatment of those held prisoner by U.S. forces.

Five: *From 'W' to Dubya*
This is an attempt at a humorous view of the troubling tenure of President George W. Bush.

Six: *QUIA IX XI MMI: New Wars on Old Dust*
A poem relating dust—that which rose from the piles of debris the Twin Towers became and that which man will return to—to the so-called post-nine/eleven era. The capitalized portion of the title is Latin for *'since 9/11/2001.'*

Seven: *Ponderings of a Trapped Soldier*
The thoughts, presumably the last ones, of a soldier pinned down in the rubble and ruins of a shelled building.

Eight: *Caravan*
A description of a brief encounter, made in the middle of the desert, between two very different cultures.

Nine: *A Truth Discovered Before Dying*
That truth is, perhaps, that things are not always what they are believed to have been.

Ten: *Painting of a Horse*
This poem derives from a dream an old girlfriend had in which a painting of horse was the most stirring element. Anything else that one can extract from the poem is left to one's own imagination.

Eleven: *And Great Was Its Fall*
A sort of warning that fate turns quickly for the vain and ill prepared. The title comes from a Bible verse that I liked.

Twelve: *Onward*
This is a short tale of a man who has come to define himself, at least partially, by the leg injury he sustained in war.

Thirteen: *Bill and George*
An attempt at making a humorous contrast between the 42nd and 43rd Presidents of the United States,

Fourteen: *Carlton*
The story of Major League Baseball pitcher Steve Carlton is a kind of sad one in the end. Carlton, who gained superstar status while playing for the Philadelphia Phillies, ranks among the greatest pitchers in baseball history

but the last two years of his career were ones in which he made a fool of himself, proving that the time to stop something comes even the great ones. Carlton also became a very strange man in retirement, and gave one of the most bizarre interviews I have ever read.

Fifteen: *Pennsylvania Avenue*
To the tune of the Beatles' "Penny Lane."

Sixteen: *The Terrorist*
The word terrorist has become so overused; it is a black comedy onto itself.

Seventeen: *Ruben Soto*
The ill-fated protagonist is a poor soul who knows no better than to join the Army and fight a silly war. The name was culled from a story of a real soldier who died in the early days of the Iraq. The story, however, is completely invented and is used only to illustrate the horrors of war. I found inspiration for the poem in the e.e. cummings' work which begins "I sing of Olaf glad and big . . ."

Eighteen: *Come to Ol' Baghdad*
A humorous look at the place the Western World has been staring at for the past three years, waiting for the paint to dry there.

Nineteen: *Hinges*
This poem explores the evolution of a bad idea. It asks a sort of a tail-wagging-the-dog question. And I'll leave the readers to figure the rest of it out.

Twenty: *Gefilte Fish*
The poem looks at the two primary uses of the tongue by juxtaposing the taste and the meaning of the traditional Passover staple.

Twenty-One: *Shards*
A look at what is left over—in many ways—after war has taken our better thinking and reduced it to shards.

Twenty-Two: *My Wedding at Borders*
This is an abstract look at my wedding, to Danila Tello, at the coffee shop in Borders bookstore in Greensboro, NC (in October 2005), the very site at which we met eight months earlier.

Twenty-Three: *Water*
Think of water as a metaphor for abundance and things taken for granted, particularly in the final verse when it is gone.

Twenty-Four: *In Peru*
Our (Danila and I) honeymoon was spent in various parts of Peru, Danila's native country. This poem is a tribute to my wife's homeland. I was very much taken aback by the people during my time in Peru. The people are at once proud, resigned to the constant nuisance of their grind and incredibly industrious.

Twenty-Five: *The King of a Small Castle*
This poem was written a few days after my father died, in January 2006. Its title comes from the fact that we—my 12 siblings and I—were raised in a 900 square-foot house, which my father ruled over with an iron fist. My father later became a more loving man in his old age but I had long since left home by then. But the poem is mostly about the little-seen complexities contained in the man my father was. A man, alas, I did not know well.

Twenty-Six: *USS Ranger . . . The Philippine Islands*
I wrote the original draft of this poem in the late-1980s while recalling my time at sea in the U.S. Navy in the early '80s and the week or so we spent in port what we called the PI. Subic Bay (or Pubic Bay, as it was sometimes referred) was a typical port city where decadence was very much in fashion.

Twenty-Seven: *Heaven*
I wish I believed in Heaven and Jesus and God and things related to the afterlife. But I don't.

Twenty-Eight: *Turning*
A simple poem that plays on the old them, "The older I get, the less I know."

Twenty-Nine: *Up Is Down*
This poem attempts to put the "reasonableness" of war in the same category as the other things mentioned. It's hard to swim in the air.

Thirty: *The Journalist*
I wrote this as a nod to my so-called 'day job' as a newspaperman.

Thirty-One: *Wife*
This poem is really some simple meanderings on a few possible ways of looking at the mighty feminine, which is almost always the better half.

Thirty-Two: *27 Carolina Avenue*
This is the address of the house in which I grew up. It is, therefore, the "small castle" over which my father ruled. The poem recalls a kind of real event. A friend of mine (who was actually a male friend) came to visit me once and when he looked around at my parents and siblings, I could see he was amazed. At one time sixteen people lived in the house; me, my 12 siblings, my parents and my father's aunt Anne. The year before I left home in 1979, 15 people lived there, a group that included my sister Patty and her family of six.

Jim McNally
336-471-0507 (CELL)

Made in the USA
Columbia, SC
23 November 2021